This book belongs to

....

It was given to me by

....

On this date

....

MARY & ME
Devotions for Girls

Trisha White
Priebe

BARBOUR **kidz**

A Division of Barbour Publishing

To Aurora and Evie

May this little book be a constant reminder that you are loved and supported as you grow up to become women who stay faithful to God *no matter what*.

Cover illustrations by Pedro Riquelme

Published by Barbour Publishing, Inc., 1810 Barbour Drive, Uhrichsville, Ohio 44683, www.barbourbooks.com

Our mission is to inspire the world with the life-changing message of the Bible.

 Member of the Evangelical Christian Publishers Association

Printed in China.

002013 0524 DS

Welcome to
MARY & ME
Devotions for Girls!

You hold in your hands the exciting story of a courageous and faithful girl chosen by God for an important job.

You'll see the surprise visit by an angel...the humble stable where Mary gave birth...the miracles she witnessed and the trials she faced...and you will be captivated by her unwavering love and devotion. Jesus was so much more than Mary's son; He was her Savior.

With each turn of the page, you will discover that God had something special for Mary to do—and He has something special for *you* to do, as well. Your life has an important purpose in God's big plan.

Let Mary's courage inspire you to trust Jesus and to believe that you, too, can be used to point those around you to God's glory.

This is a story of love, hope, and the strength found in the heart of a girl chosen by God to help change the world forever.

CHOSEN GIRL

A LOWLY BEGINNING

"The Lord has looked on me,
His servant-girl and one
who is not important."
LUKE 1:48

In your hands, you hold the wild and wonderful story of a woman whose life helped shape the course of history. That's right! *Your* life has been changed because of *her* life.

Who are we talking about? Mary, of course!

In Galilee, a quiet region surrounded by rolling hills and fields of golden wheat, lived a young teenager named Mary. She lived a simple life in a small town that was nothing fancy. The fact that Mary wasn't known for anything outstanding is part of what makes her story so very special. God loved her and chose her for one very important purpose.

Maybe you wonder if God has a big job for you to do when you grow up. If so, Mary would want you to keep reading. She never could have imagined what wonderful things God had planned for her life.

Let the words of this book carry you away to a place where miracles unfold and where the ordinary becomes the extraordinary!

Let's see what happens next.

God, thank You for putting Mary's story in the Bible so I can read and learn from it. Thank You for her life. Amen.

AN IMPORTANT VISIT

*The angel came to her and said,
"You are honored very much.
You are a favored woman. The
Lord is with you. You are chosen
from among many women."*
LUKE 1:28

Maybe it was early one afternoon that something incredible happened. Or maybe it was late in an evening when stars painted the velvety night sky.

The Bible tells us that suddenly a great angel of light appeared before Mary!

Can you imagine?

Mary must have wondered if she were dreaming. She might have even glanced at the door, wondering if she should call for help.

Then this angel, whose name was Gabriel, said these words: "Mary, do not be afraid. You have found favor with God. See! You are to become a mother and have a Son. You are to give Him the name Jesus. He will be great" (Luke 1:30–32).

For sure, Mary was confused by now. She was engaged to be married to a man named Joseph, but they hadn't had their wedding yet.

Gabriel explained that nothing was too difficult for God.

So Mary had an important choice to make. Would she believe this messenger from heaven? Or would she think this was just a dream and forget it ever happened?

What would you do?

God, thank You that nothing is impossible with You. You cared about Mary's story, and You care about mine. Amen.

A WILLING SERVANT

Then Mary said, "I am willing to be used of the Lord. Let it happen to me as you have said." Then the angel went away from her.
LUKE 1:38

As Gabriel's words echoed through the air, Mary knew she must decide.

On one hand, she loved God and wanted to please Him. On the other hand, what would people think? How would they react to the news?

Ever since she was a little girl, Mary had listened to the tales of the ancient prophecy—passed down through generations—which spoke of a wonderful and mighty Savior, a Messiah who would bring hope and peace to the land.

The idea of becoming the mother of Jesus must have been

- *scary*
- *exciting*
- *shocking*
- *wonderful*

Yet she told the angel that she was a willing servant of the Lord.

Did you know that you, too, can be a willing servant of God? Like Mary, you must trust God's plan for your life and eagerly follow where He leads, knowing He has chosen you to do something special.

Overwhelmed with joy, Mary knew in her heart that something truly wonderful was about to happen. Jesus was on the way!

Let's keep reading.

God, just as You had
a plan for Mary's life,
You have a good plan for
me. Help me trust You.
Amen.

A BEAUTIFUL SONG

Then Mary said, "My heart sings with thanks for my Lord."
LUKE 1:46

Her heart bursting with joy at the news that Jesus was coming to save the world, Mary decided to visit her older cousin Elizabeth.

After taking the long and tiring journey, she greeted her cousin, and something remarkable happened. Elizabeth too was going to have a baby. Her baby jumped for joy when Mary came near. Even Elizabeth's unborn baby knew that Jesus was important.

Overwhelmed by God's kindness, Mary burst into song, her voice carrying the weight of centuries of praise from thousands of believers before her who had waited in anticipation for the arrival of Jesus.

Mary's song would be called "the Magnificat," and it was filled with the promises of God.

Mary and Elizabeth must have sat together—their hands cradling their growing bellies—sharing stories of God's goodness and filling the room with laughter as they anticipated how He would keep His promises.

If you were going to write a song about God, what would you say? What would you call your song?

God, thank You for
being so good that I
could fill a song with
joyful truths about You.
You are always worthy
of praise. Amen.

A BRAVE
MOM

A ROAD TRIP

In those days Caesar Augustus sent out word that the name of every person in the Roman nation must be written in the books of the nation.
LUKE 2:1

Mary and Joseph's simple life was upset when news arrived from a distant land: a census was underway. A census means that everyone in the whole country had to be counted.

For Mary and Joseph, this meant traveling to the town of Bethlehem, where Joseph's family came from.

They packed a few things, climbed onto the back of their trusty donkey, and began their trip.

Soon, the ancient town of Bethlehem appeared in the distance, nestled among the hills.

The air was filled with anticipation as exhausted travelers began looking for places to stay.

Unfortunately, the village was overflowing with visitors.

Knowing Mary was uncomfortable and the baby was soon to be born, Joseph searched for a place where they could stay and Mary could rest. But each time, he received the same reply: "I'm sorry. We're full. No room here."

What would *you* have done? Would you have trusted that God still had a plan?

What happened next was nothing short of amazing.

God, I know that
even when it looks as if
things are going wrong,
You are still in control.
I can trust You. Amen.

A HUMBLE BIRTH

While they were there in Bethlehem, the time came for Mary to give birth to her baby.
LUKE 2:6

Finally, someone took pity on Mary and Joseph and said they could stay in their old, humble stable—perhaps a cave carved out of rock—where the donkeys and other animals were kept.

And there, in the quiet of the night—in the place she least expected it to happen—Mary gave birth to the baby who would change the world.

She named Him *Jesus*, just as the angel Gabriel had said.

As the baby's cries echoed through the stable, Mary looked at her son with eyes filled with love and wonder. She wrapped Him in soft cloth and laid Him in a manger because there was no crib.

God had chosen a humble girl to give birth in a humble stable to the humble King. Jesus didn't come to be served— He came *to serve.*

Would you rather be helped or help others? Mary and Jesus gave us a wonderful example of loving and helping others.

But the story isn't over. Far from it. So let's keep reading.

God, thank You for giving us the greatest gift—Your Son, Jesus. Thank You for sending Him on that first Christmas Day. Amen.

A FULL HEART

*All who heard it were surprised
at what the shepherds told them.
But Mary hid all these words in her
heart. She thought about them much.*
Luke 2:18–19

Shortly after Jesus was born, shepherds appeared in the doorway of the stable, excited to see the new baby.

They must have fallen to their knees, overwhelmed with gratitude and wonder as they worshipped the miracle in the manger.

Time stood still as Mary introduced this little baby they had all hoped to see in their lifetime. Can you imagine how the shepherds' hearts must have burst with joy as they shared how the angel had told them of Jesus' birth and then how the whole sky had filled with angels praising God?

When the shepherds left to share their news with others, Mary treasured all these moments in her heart. From the time she had accepted God's good plan for her life, she had faced doubts, criticisms, and challenges. Yet God had been faithful to her. And as she held her newborn son, she understood God would continue to be faithful.

Mary's heart was full of hope. What has God done for you that fills your heart with joy?

God, thank You for filling
my heart with hope. You are
the one I love most. Help
me love You more. Amen.

A DRAMATIC ESCAPE

When they had gone, an angel of the Lord came to Joseph in a dream. He said, "Get up. Take the young Child and His mother to the country of Egypt. Go as fast as you can! Stay there until you hear from Me. Herod is going to look for the young Child to kill Him."
MATTHEW 2:13

When Jesus was a little bit older, wise men came to worship Him. Opening their bags of riches, they gave Him gold and perfume and spices. What a wonderful visit it must have been!

But later that night, Joseph had a dream. He was visited by an angel who told him to get up and take Mary and Jesus to the country of Egypt as fast as possible, because an evil ruler named Herod wanted to kill Jesus.

They gathered everything they owned, and Mary wrapped Jesus in a warm blanket. Then she and Joseph left, under the shimmering light of the moon. How Mary's heart must have been sad, but—as she had done from the very beginning—she trusted God to lead her.

Through valleys and across rivers, she pressed on with her family, making the exciting escape into Egypt, where they lived until Herod died.

Sometimes we obey God in small things. At other times, we obey Him in bigger things. But always we should seek to obey Him, no matter what.

God, help me always obey You—in big and small ways. You know what is best for me. Amen.

A FOLLOWER
OF JESUS

A LOST SON

They thought Jesus was with the others of the group. They walked for one day. Then they looked for Him among their family and friends. When they could not find Jesus, they turned back to Jerusalem to look for Him.
Luke 2:44–45

The Bible doesn't tell us much about Mary's life when Jesus was a child. But when Jesus was twelve years old, Mary and Joseph took Him on another journey—this time to Jerusalem to celebrate how God had led the Jews out of slavery in Egypt.

They enjoyed this trip as they did every year, and then they headed home with the other travelers in their group.

For an entire day, Joseph and Mary walked, laughing with their friends and singing the joyful hymns of their people. Then they decided to check on Jesus.

But they couldn't find Him anywhere. Why wasn't He with His friends?

Imagine the panic that must have seized Mary's heart! Her eyes frantically searched the crowds. "Have you seen my son?" she must have asked.

But the answer was always *no*.

Three long, scary days later, she and Joseph found Jesus in the temple, sitting with the wisest teachers in the land.

"We were so scared!" Mary exclaimed.

Jesus replied, "Do you not know that I must be in My Father's house?"

Mary *didn't* understand, but it would all become clear one day.

God, give me the
courage Jesus had to
do the right thing even
when it doesn't make
sense to others. Amen.

AN EXCITING WEDDING

Three days later there was a wedding in the town of Cana in the country of Galilee. The mother of Jesus was there.
JOHN 2:1

Years later, in the village of Cana, a young couple gathered everyone together for their big day. Weddings were a big deal, and this one was no exception.

Mary was there with Jesus, who was a grown man by this time.

But the laughter and joy of the wedding were soon interrupted when word reached the bride and groom that they had run out of the best drink.

That was embarrassing.

Mary—her heart brimming with compassion for the couple—said to Jesus, "You can fix this!" She knew He could do anything.

Soon, Jesus told the servants to fill six large stone jars with water. And then He turned the water into the most delicious drink anyone had ever tasted.

This was Jesus' first miracle, and Mary was there for it. She was the first to believe He could do it, and she was right. She put her trust in Him and was not disappointed.

Have you ever asked God to do something big? Do you believe He could do it?

God, teach me to come to You first when I need help. You can do anything. Amen.

A HORRIBLE NIGHT

Jesus saw His mother and the follower whom He loved standing near. He said to His mother, "Woman, look at your son."
JOHN 19:26

More than anyone in the world, Mary got to witness the extraordinary life and ministry of Jesus from His birth to His miracles to His ministry.

But this privilege also came with a price.

She was also a witness to the horrible day Jesus died.

Theirs was a special, unbreakable bond between a mother and her son.

While Jesus was on the cross, He called out to His dear friend John and asked him to care for Mary. This response showed Jesus' love for His mother, even as He was dying.

And at risk of her own life, Mary stood at the foot of the cross, unwilling to abandon her son in His greatest pain.

The ground trembled and the sky grew dark. The world became absolutely still, and what may have felt like deep, never-ending sadness filled Mary's heart.

The one she loved more than her own life had died.

What happened next would be almost too good to be true. But God is good at going beyond our expectations, isn't He?

God, when I am expected
to do something hard,
help me to have courage,
like Mary. Amen.

A HOPEFUL MORNING

Early in the morning on the first day of the week, the women went to the grave taking the spices they had made ready. They found the stone had been pushed away from the grave. They went in but they did not find the body of the Lord Jesus.
LUKE 24:1–3

After Jesus died, the world held its breath in anticipation of what God would do to fix what had happened to Jesus and forever change the course of history.

The tomb where Jesus was buried stood silent and still.

His followers—including His mother, Mary—were filled with sadness.

But as the first rays of dawn scattered their sunbeams on the third morning after His death, the women went to the tomb. . .and found the stone that sealed the door rolled away. Now there was just an empty space where Jesus' body had been. Two angels asked the women why they looked for the living among the dead.

Jesus was risen! This was the first Easter.

Some Bible teachers believe Mary, the mother of Jesus, is described as "the mother of the younger James and of Joses" (Mark 15:40) and was one of the women who found the tomb empty.

Can you imagine how she must have gone from the deepest sadness to the greatest joy? Jesus was alive! Because of that, Mary had hope—and so do *you*.

God, when I am sad,
help me always to have
hope in You. You always
have a good plan. Amen.

AN EXAMPLE
FOR ALL

A STRONG FAITH

"You are happy because you believed. Everything will happen as the Lord told you it would happen."
Luke 1:45

From the very beginning, Mary accepted her special job as the mother of Jesus with great courage and faith. She wasn't perfect—she was human like you and me—but she was faithful.